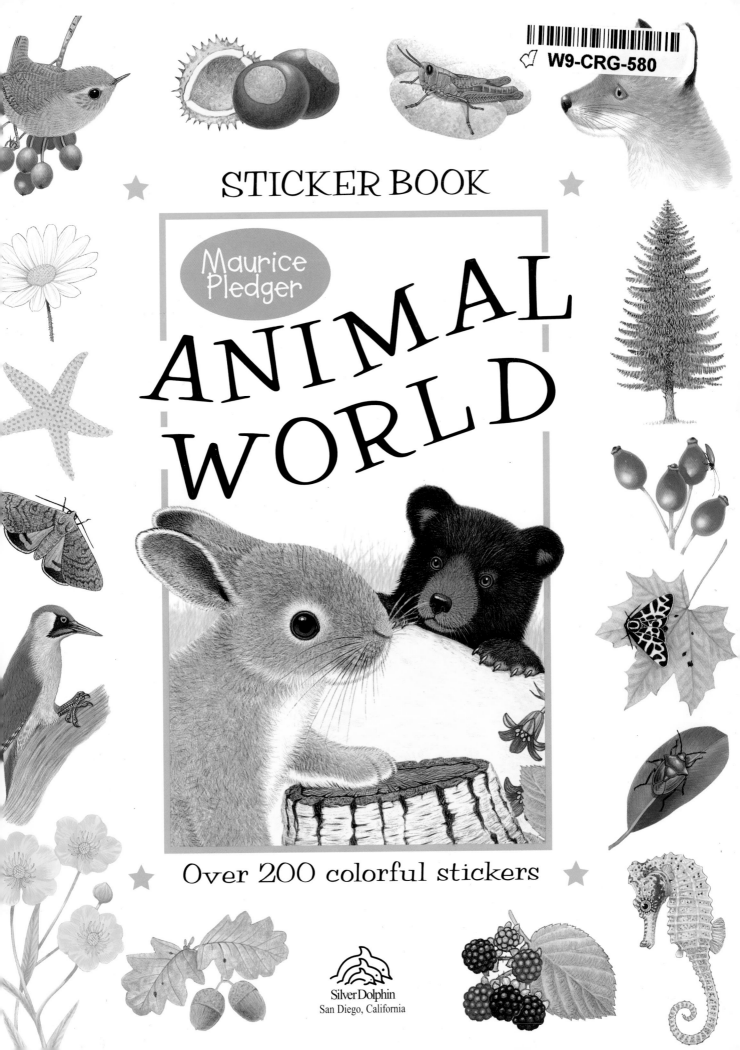

STICKER BOOK

Maurice Pledger

ANIMAL WORLD

Over 200 colorful stickers

Silver Dolphin
San Diego, California

Silver Dolphin

Silver Dolphin Books
An imprint of the Baker & Taylor Publishing Group
10350 Barnes Canyon Road, San Diego, CA 92121
www.silverdolphinbooks.com

This edition published in 2010
First edition published in 2002

ISBN-13: 978-1-60710-167-3
ISBN-10: 1-60710-167-X

Made in Malaysia

2 3 4 5 14 13 12 11 10

About this book

Get ready to be a sticker collector! On the following pages you can learn about the many different places where animals live—from grassy meadows to sandy seashores.

Turn to the back of the book, and you'll find lots of stickers, too. Use them to complete the sticker activities on every page by filling in the animal shapes or making up your own pictures of the wonderful world of animals.

Different faces in different places

Look at the animals in this picture. Harry Hare lives in the grassy meadow. Oscar Otter and Sally Cygnet like to stay near the river. And Elly Eagle spends her time high in the mountains. Can you guess where Olivia Owl and Dilly Dormouse make their home?

In this book you'll meet all sorts of wonderful creatures and find out about the different places, or **habitats**, where they live—and don't forget to have fun using your stickers as you go!

★ All around the MEADOW

Morris Mouse and his family live in the grassy meadow. You can find out about some of the other plants and animals that live there on the next few pages, but first use your stickers to add another mouse and a poppy to the scene.

Who lives in the meadow?

Morris Mouse has lots of animal friends in the grassy meadow where he lives. Look for them the next time you're out walking in the fields.

Pheasant

Swallow

Meadow pippit

Skylark

Quail

Use your stickers to fill in the shapes with the right creatures. You can fill them all in now or wait until you see each different one.

Rabbit

Hare

Deer

male

female

Grass snake

Weasel

More meadow friends

See how many of these creepy-crawlies you can find next time you're in a meadow on a sunny summer's day.

Butterflies

Ladybugs

Cinnabar moth

Fly

Wasp

Bumblebee

Spider

Snail

Beetle

Caterpillar

Grasshopper

Shield bug

Lots of different plants grow in meadows.
They provide food for many of the creatures
that live alongside them.

Poppy

Daisies

Grass

Wheat

Buttercups

Now
TURN THE PAGE
and make your own
meadow picture using
your stickers.

All around the WOOD

The shady wood is home to lots of secretive creatures, like Olivia Owl. Use your stickers to add a wood mouse and another toadstool to the scene, then turn the page to find out more about these woodland creatures.

Who lives in the wood?

Olivia Owl is out exploring her woodland home. Do you know the names of any of the creatures she has found?

Beetles

Moths

Ants

Slug

Badger

Wood lice

Fox

Say their names as you fill in their shapes
with your stickers.

Blue tit

Jackdaw

Wren

Wood pigeon

Woodpecker

Squirrel

Bat

Dormouse

Wood mouse

17

What grows in the wood?

Fall is a great time to go looking for interesting woodland plants—look for colorful berries, nuts, and toadstools. In the spring you might find a beautiful carpet of bluebells covering the ground.

Horse chestnut

Holly

Blackberries

Bluebells

Toadstools

REMEMBER, never eat any of the plants you find, however tasty they may look. Some of them can make you very sick!

Leaves

Acorns

Sycamore seeds

Now TURN THE PAGE and make your own woodland scene of Olivia Owl and her friends.

Fir cone

Rose hips

Dog roses

19

All around the RIVER

Oscar Otter spends most of his time down by the river, hunting for a tasty fish to eat! Add stickers of a heron and some rushes to the picture, then turn the page to find out more about Oscar's riverbank friends.

Down by the water!

Look for these waterbirds when you're near rivers and lakes. Herons often stand in shallow water for hours without moving in an effort to catch a fish!

Kingfisher

Wagtail

Swan

Heron

Cygnet

Use your stickers to fill in these shapes with some more riverbank plants and animals.

Salmon

Beaver

Darter dragonfly

Water vole

Mayfly

Cattails

Reeds

Now
TURN THE PAGE
and make up your own
picture of life on the
riverbank.

All around the POND

Dora Duckling and her brothers and sisters love to go exploring down on the pond. Use your stickers to add another water lily and a terrapin to the scene, then turn the page to learn all about the creatures that live there.

What's in the pond?

Dora Duckling likes to dabble and dive to see what's going on under the surface of the pond.
All sorts of interesting creatures live there—you can see some of them here.

Frog

Tadpoles

Frog spawn

Water beetle

Newt

Water strider

Toad

Terrapin

Use your stickers to fill in the shapes with these other pond dwellers.

Water lily

Pondweed

Pond snails

Dragonfly nymph

Hawker dragonfly

Stickleback

Now
TURN THE PAGE
and use your stickers to
make your own picture of
life in the depths of
the pond.

Minnows

All around the SEASHORE

What has Sidney Seal found down on the beach? Use your stickers to add a crab and some sea holly to the picture, then turn the page to see what else Sidney has discovered on his travels.

Down on the beach!

How many of these things have you seen when you've been at the beach? Look for them along the shore and in rock pools.

Seagull

Shrimp

Oystercatcher

Crab

Sea horse

Fish

Sea holly

Starfish

Use your stickers to fill in the shapes with things that you have found by the sea.

Sea anemone

Sea urchin

Coral

Mermaid's purse

Barnacles

Seaweed

Sand dollar

Now
TURN THE PAGE
and use your stickers
to make your own
deep-sea scene.

Shells

All around the MOUNTAIN

Larry Lynx loves his home high up in the mountains. Turn the page to see some of the other interesting creatures that live there—but first add a chipmunk and another fir tree to the scene.

⭐ Up on the mountain!

Here are some of Larry Lynx's mountain friends. Many of them are hard to spot because they are white like the snowy mountaintops!

Snowy owl

Ptarmigan

Mountain lion

Kestrel

Eagle

Wolf

Mountain goat

Use your stickers to fill in the shapes with these other mountain plants and animals.

Fir tree

Ferns

Stoat

Lichen

Marmot

Chipmunk

NOW
TURN THE PAGE
and make your own
mountain scene using
your stickers.

Brown bear

Now see if you can remember the
names of all the creatures in this scene.
If you can't, look back through the book to remind
yourself—and don't forget to look for them
the next time you're on a nature walk.

How to use your stickers

Look for the page numbers on the sticker sheets to help you find the right stickers for the different activities in this book. Peel each one carefully from its backing sheet and use it to fill in the shapes or add to the pictures. You can also use your stickers to record the animals you see in real life. Look for the creatures in this book when you're outside, then fill in their sticker shapes as you see them. Some animals are easier to spot than others. Some may not live where you do, so look for them when you visit the zoo. Soon you'll find your whole book is complete. Then you'll be a champion sticker collector!

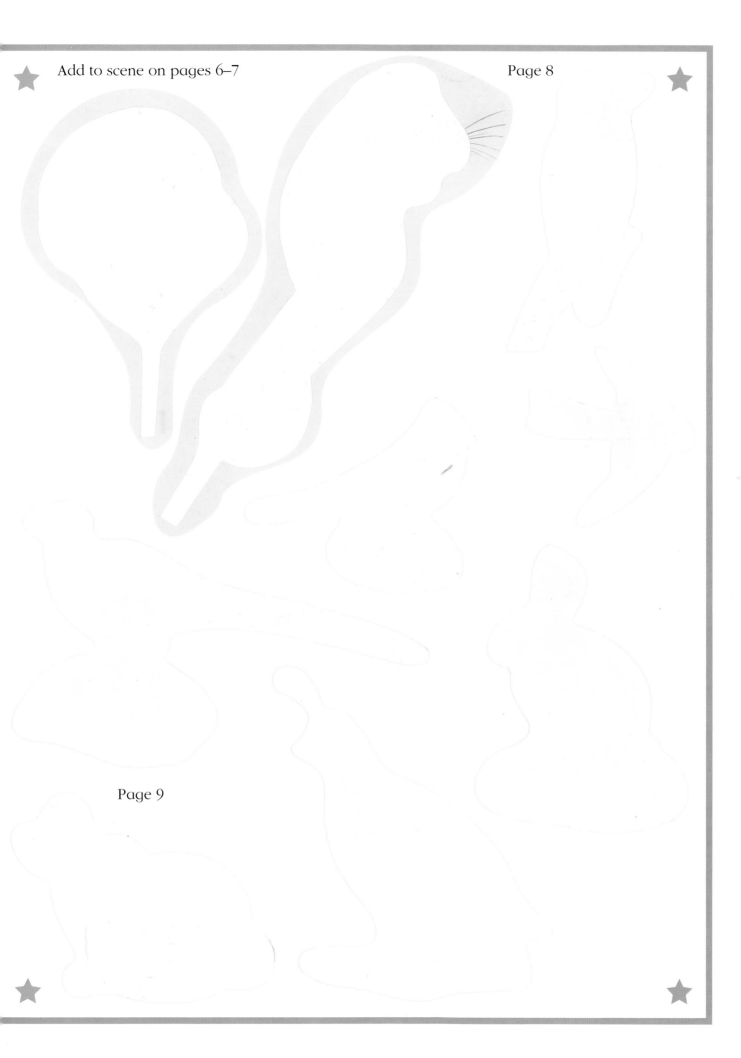

Page 9

Page 9

Page 10

Add to scene on pages 12–13

Add to scene on pages 12–13

Add to scene on pages 14–15

Page 16

Page 17

Page 19

Add to scene on pages 20–21

Add to scene on pages 20–21

Add to scene on pages 22–23

Page 24

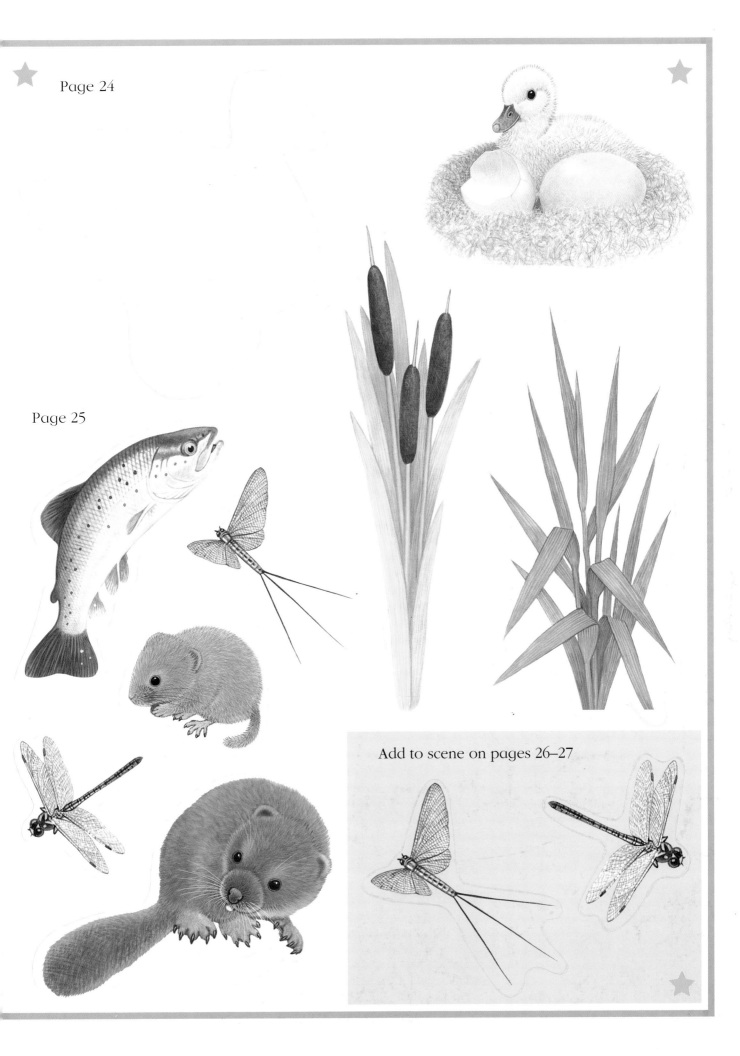

Page 24

Page 25

Add to scene on pages 26–27

Add to scene on pages 26–27

Add to scene on pages 28–29

Page 30

Page 31

Add to scene on pages 32–33

Add to scene on pages 34–35

Page 36

Page 37

Add to scene on pages 38–39

Add to scene on pages 40–41

Page 42

Page 43

Add to scene on pages 44–45